Dear Parents,

I would like to suggest that reading can be a great substitute for electronic games. If your child learns a non-native language, it will open up his horizon to the world and motivate his desire to learn even more languages, allowing him to discover the entirety of our world.

As an Arabic native speaker, an English teacher, and a Spanish language student, I am motivated to publish this book. I encourage you to introduce your children to this series so that they can learn more languages through their favorite reading.

Thank you for your time and consideration.

Sincerely,
Author

Estimados padres,

Me gustaría sugerir que la lectura puede ser un gran sustituto de los juegos electrónicos. Si su hijo aprende un idioma no nativo, abrirá su horizonte al mundo y motivará su deseo de aprender aún más idiomas, permitiéndole descubrir la totalidad de nuestro mundo.

Como hablante nativo de árabe, profesor de inglés y estudiante de español, estoy motivado para publicar este libro. Os animo a introducir a vuestros hijos a esta serie para que puedan aprender más idiomas a través de su lectura favorita.

Gracias por su tiempo y consideración.

Atentamente,
Autor

الآباء الأعزاء،

أود أن أقترح أن القراءة يمكن أن تكون بديلاً رائعًا للألعاب الإلكترونية. إذا تعلم طفلك لغة غير أصلية ، فسوف يفتح ذلك أفقه على العالم ويحفز رغبته في تعلم المزيد من اللغات ، مما يسمح له باكتشاف عالمنا بأكمله.

بصفتي متحدثًا للغة العربية ، ومعلمًا للغة الإنجليزية ، ومتعلمًا للغة الإسبانية ، فإنني متحمس لنشر هذا الكتاب. أشجعك على تعريف أطفالك بهذه السلسلة حتى يتمكنوا من تعلم المزيد من اللغات من خلال قراءتهم المفضلة.

شكرا لك على وقتك واحترامك.

بإخلاص،
المؤلف

During the Corona pandemic, people communicated through social networking sites when the world entered partial or complete lockdown.

Three kids from three different countries had to form a Trio.

The three children agreed that each one of them would learn the language of the other two so that this friendship would last and develop.

This book documents how each of these three children learned two additional language.

Durante la pandemia de coronavirus, la gente se comunicaba a través de las redes sociales cuando el mundo entró en un confinamiento parcial o total.

Tres niños de tres países diferentes tuvieron que formar un trío.

Los tres niños acordaron que cada uno de ellos aprendería el idioma de los otros dos para que esta amistad perdurara y se desarrollara.

Este libro documenta cómo cada uno de estos tres niños aprendió dos idiomas adicionales.

خلال جائحة كورونا، تواصل الناس عبر مواقع التواصل الاجتماعي عندما دخل العالم في حظر جزئي أو كامل.

كان على ثلاثة أطفال من ثلاث دول مختلفة أن يشكلوا صداقة ثلاثية.
اتفق الأطفال الثلاثة على أن يتعلم كل واحد منهم لغة الاثنين الآخرين حتى تستمر هذه الصداقة وتتطور.

يوثق هذا الكتاب كيف تعلم كل من هؤلاء الأطفال الثلاثة لغتين إضافيتين.

speaking for the first time

Hablando por primera vez

attahadduth le'awal marrah

التَّحَدُّث لِأَوْلِ مَرَّة

Hello
Welcome

Hola
Bienvenido

مرحبا
Marhaba
أهلا وسهلا
Ahlan wa Sahlan

Let's start
getting to know
each other

Empecemos
a conocernos

لِنَبْدَأَ التعارف
lenabd'a
atta'aruf

What is your name?
I am Oliver.

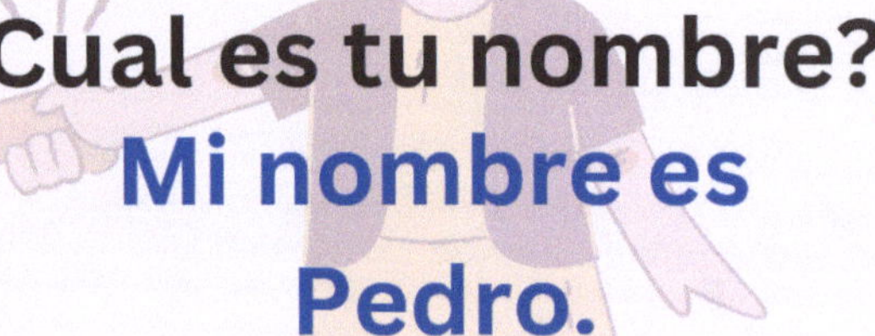

Cual es tu nombre?
Mi nombre es
Pedro.

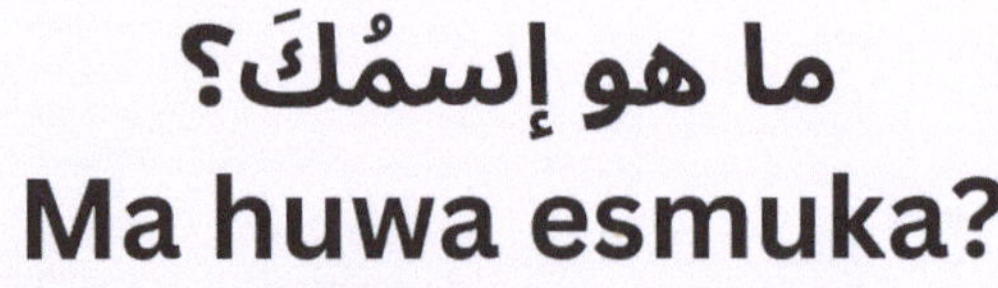

ما هو إسمُكَ؟
Ma huwa esmuka?
إسمي محمّد.
Esmi Mohammed.

How are you?

I am fine,
thank you.

¿Cómo estás?

Estoy bien,
gracias.

كَيفَ حالُكَ؟
kaifa haluka
أنا بخير, شُكْراً
Ana bekhair, shukran

Nice to meet you.
Nice to meet you too.

Mucho gusto.
Mucho gusto también.

سعيد بلقائك
Sa'eed belqa'ek.
سعيد بلقائك أيضاً
Sa'eed belqa'ek aydan.

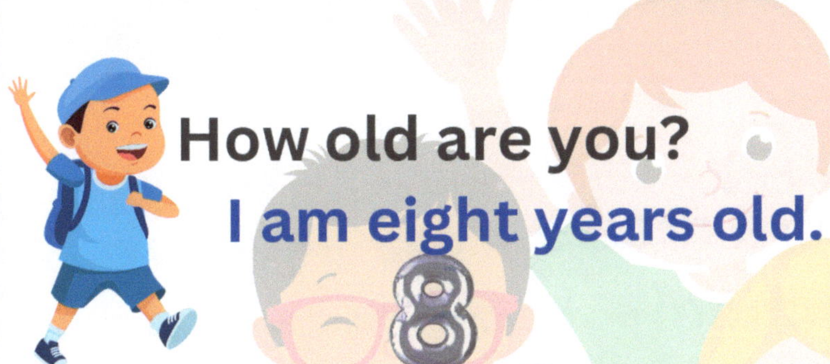

How old are you?
I am eight years old.
8

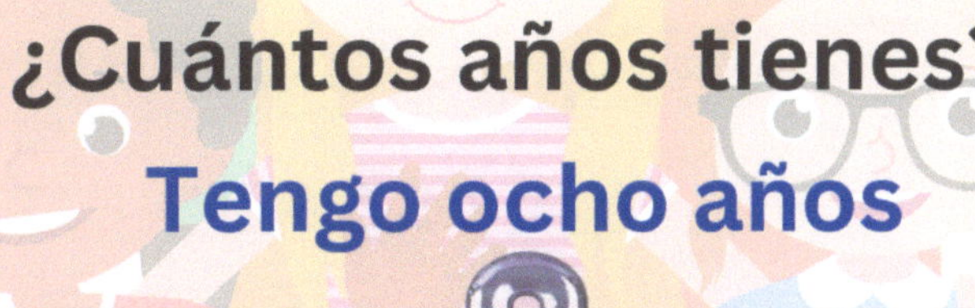

¿Cuántos años tienes?
Tengo ocho años
8

كم عمرك؟
Kam umruka?
عمري ثمان سنوات
umri thaman sanawat
8

Where do you study?
**I study in the third grade
of primary school**

¿Donde estudias?
**Estudio en tercer
grado de primaria.**

I have two friends,
Pedro and Mohammed.

Tengo dos amigos
Oliver y Mohammed.

لدي صديقان
ladaya sadiqan
أليفر و بيدرو
Oliver wa Pedro.

Numbers

Números

الأرقام
al'arqam

Let's count
1- One
2- Two
3- Three

Vamos a conter
1- uno
2- dos
3- tres

دَعْنا نَعُدُ
da'na na'udu
1- واحد Wahid
2- إثنان Ethnan
3- ثلاثة Thalatha

4- Four
5- Five
6- Six
7- Seven
8- Eight
9- Nine
10- Ten

4- Cuatro
5- Cinco
6- Seis
7- Siete
8- Ocho
9- Nueve
10- Diez

4- أربعة   4- Arba'ah
5- خمسة   5- Khamsah
6- ستة   6- sitah
7- سبعة   7 sab'ah
8- ثمانية   8- Thamaneyah
9- تسعة   9- Tis'ah
10- عشرة   10- Asharah

20- twenty	20- veinte
30- thirty	30- treinta
40- forty	40- cuarenta
50- fifty	50- cincuenta
60- sixty	60- sesenta
70- seventy	70- setenta
80- eighty	80- ochenta
90- ninety	90- noventa
100- hundred	100- ciento

عشرون -20	20- eshron
ثلاثون -30	30- thlathon
أربعون -40	40- arba'un
خمسون -50	50- khamson
ستون -60	60- setton
سبعون -70	70- sab'un
ثمانون -80	80- thmanon
تسعون -90	90- tes'un
مائة -100	100- me'ah

colors
colores
الألْوان
al'alwan

My favorite
color is blue.

Mi color favorito
es el rojo.

لوني المفضل هُوَ
lawni almufadel huwa
alakhdar الأخضر

This color is
green.

este color es
azul.

هذا اللّون هو الأحمر.
Hatha alawnu huwa'lahmar.

This color is
red.

Este color es
verde.

هذا اللّون هو الأزرق
Hatha alawnu huwa'lazraq

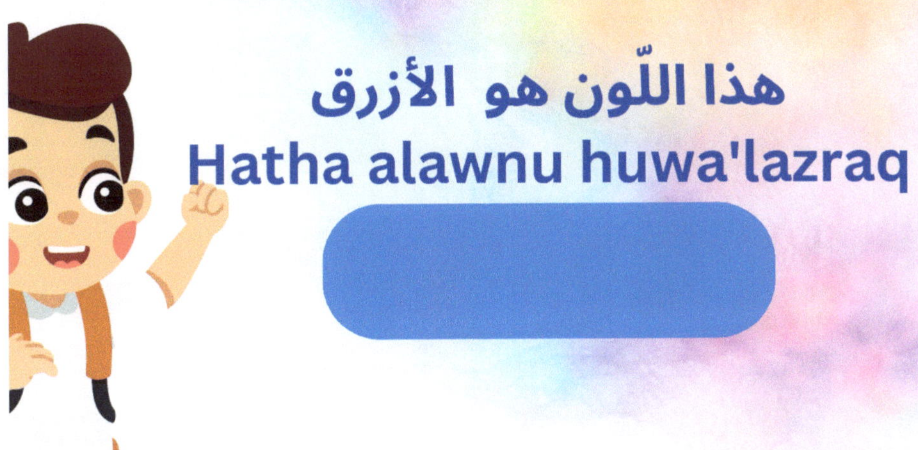

Purple Púrpura

بنفسجي

Banafsagi

Pink Rosa

وردي

Wardi

White Blanco

أبيض

Abyad

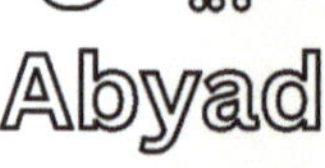

Black Negro

أسود

Aswad

Orange Naranja

برتقالي

Bortuqali

I can see
our sky
in the day is blue
and water in the lake
is blue

Puedo ver que
nuestro cielo
durante el día es
azul
y el agua del lago
es azul.

أَستطيع أن أرى

astati'u an ara

سماءَنا في النهارِ زرقاء

sama'ana finnahare zarqa'a

والمياهُ في البحيرة زرقاء

walmeyahu filbuhaira zarqa'a

Pets and animals

Mascotas y animales

alhaywanatu alaleefa الحيواناتُ الأَلِيفة
wa alhaywanat والحيوانات

Do you have pets?
I have a cat and a bird.

¿Tienes mascotas?
Tengo un gato y un perro.

هل لديكَ حيوانات؟
Hal ladaika haiwanat?

لديَّ قِطٌ وَ سَمَكَة
Ladaya qettun wa samakah

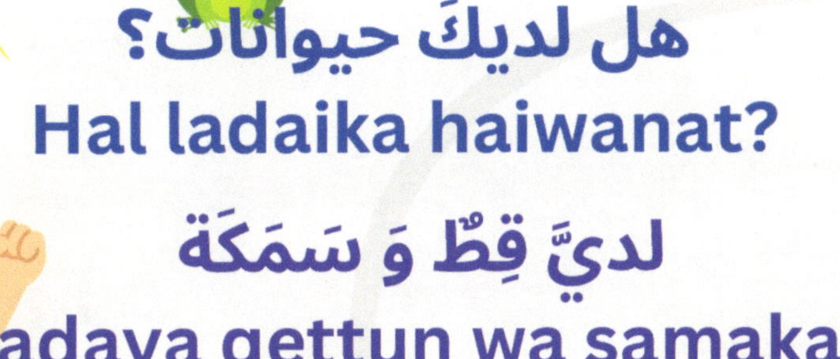
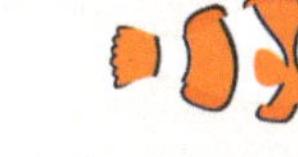

My cat saw a picture of a tiger

She got scared

She ran away

I laughed at her

Mi gata
vio una foto de un tigre

Se asustó

Se escapó

Me reí de ella

رَأَتْ قِطَّتِي صُورَةَ النِّمِر

ra'at qettati soratannemre

خَافَتْ

khafat

هَرَبَتْ

harabat

ضَحِكْتُ مِنْهَا

dhahektu menha

turtle  tortuga

سُلحَفاة

sulhafah

fish  pez

سَمَكَة

samakah

lizard  lagarto

سِحلِيَة

sehleyah

camel  camello

جَمَل

jamal

parrot  papagayo

بَبّغاء

babagha

duck  pata

بَطّة

bata

chicken pollo

دَجَاجَة

dajajah

horse caballo

حِصان

hesan

rabbit  conejo

أرنب

arnab

pigeon paloma

حَمامة

hamamah

frog rana

ضِفدَع

defda'a

bird  pájaro

طَيْر

tair

cow vaca

بَقرة

baqarah

donkey burro

حِمار

hemar

rooster  gallo

دِيك

deek

Hobbies

Pasatiempos

Hewayat هوايات

What is your favorite hobby?
My favorite hobbies are reading and football.

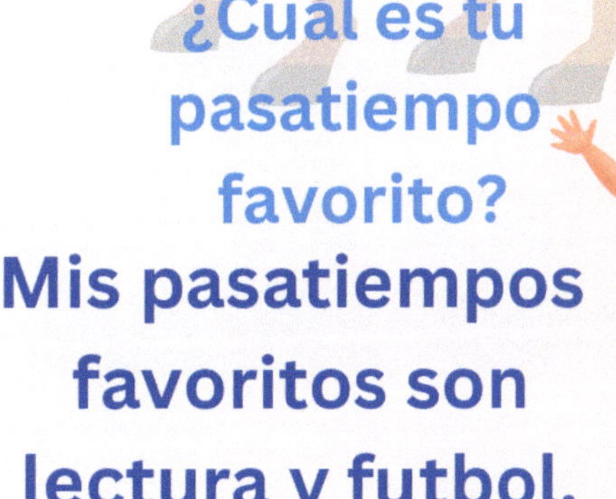

¿Cuál es tu pasatiempo favorito?
Mis pasatiempos favoritos son lectura y futbol.

Ma heya ما هِيَ hewayatuka هوايتُكَ amlmufadala المُفضلة
هواياتي المفضلة
Hewayati'lmufadalah alqera'a wa القِراءة و kuratalqadam كرة القدم

Do you need help?
I need help, please.

¿Necesitas ayuda?
Necesito ayuda, por favor.

هل تحتاج مساعدة؟
Hal tahtaj musa'ada
أحتاج مساعدة, من فضلك
Ahtaj musa'ada, men fadlek

I am an intelligent boy.
Soy un chico inteligente.
أنا ولدٌ ذكي
Ana waladun thaki

Smart boys like to read and play.

Los niños inteligentes les gusta leer y jugar.

الأطفال الأذكياء
Alatfal alathkeya'a
يحبونَ القراءةَ
Yuhebon alqera'ata
واللّعب
wala'eb

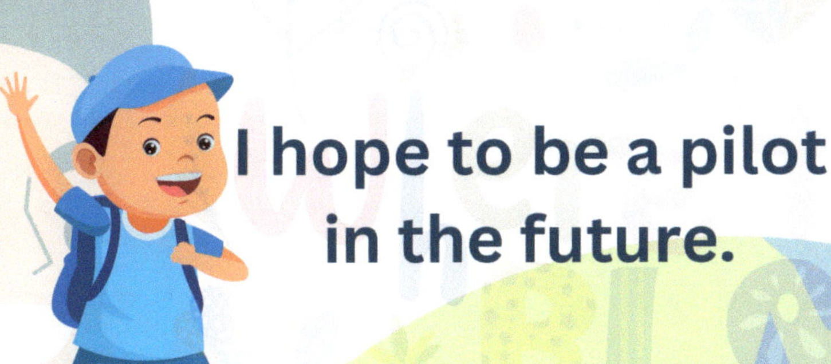

I hope to be a pilot in the future.

Espero ser piloto en el futuro.

أتمنى أن أصبحَ

Atamana an usbeha

طياراً

tayaran

في المستقبل

filmustaqbal

I'm a little child
My hopes are high
One day I'll grow up
With hard work and diligence
I'll achieve my hopes

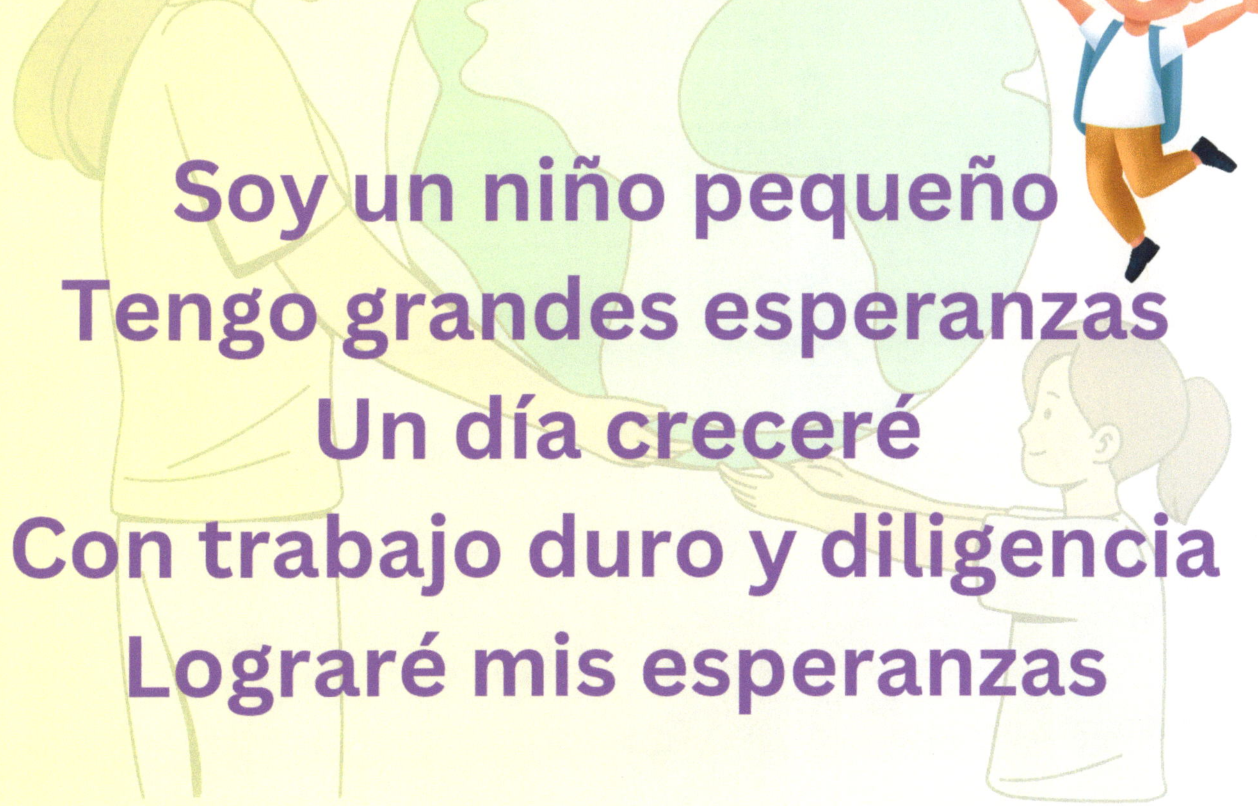

Soy un niño pequeño
Tengo grandes esperanzas
Un día creceré
Con trabajo duro y diligencia
Lograré mis esperanzas

أَنَا طِفْلٌ صغيرٌ
ana teflun sagheerun
آمالِي كَبيرة
a'amali kabeerah
يوْما مَا سَأكبُرُ
yawman ma sa'akburu
بِالجِدِ والاجْتِهادِ
beljedi wal'ejtihadi
أُحَقِقُ آمَالِي
uhaqequ a'amali

Nurse 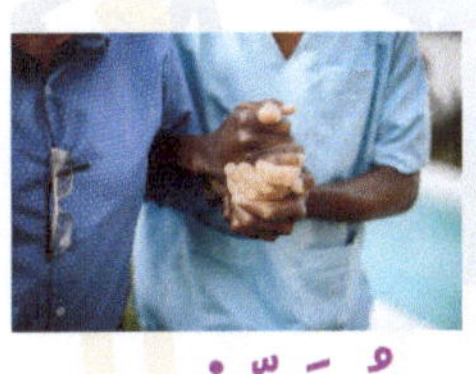 **Enfermero**

مُمَرّض
mumarredh

Engineer  **Ingeniero**

مُهندس
muhandis

Doctor 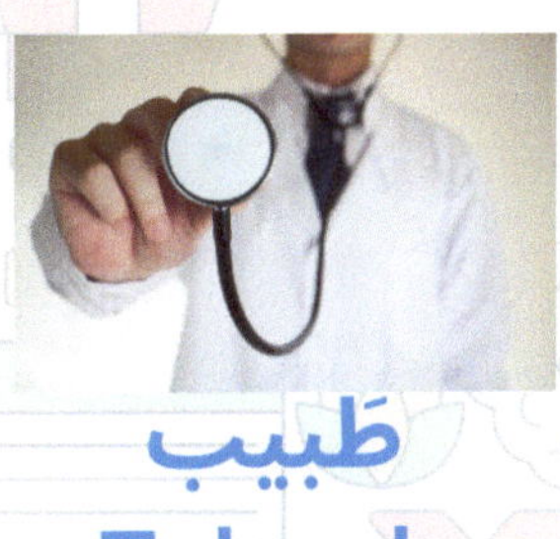 **Doctor**

طَبيب
Tabeeb

Teacher  **Maestro**

مُعلّم
Mu'alem

Worker  Obrero

عَامِل
A'amel

Fireman  Bombero

إطفائي
Etfa'ee

Farmer  Agricultor

مُزارِع
Muzare'a

Technician  Técnico

فَنّي
Fanni

With my family
Con mi familia
مَعَ عائلتي
ma'a a'elati

Please, meet my
parents.
My father and my
mother.

Por favor, conoce a
mis padres.
Mi padre y
mi madre.

تَفَضَّلْ بِلِقاءِ والديّ.
Tafaddal beleqa'e waleday.
أَبِي و أُمِّي.
Abi wa ummi.

My grandpa and my grandma

Mi abuelo y mi abuela

جَدِّي و جَدَّتِي
Jaddi wa jaddati

My sister and my brother.

Mi hermana y mi hermano.

أُختي و أخِي
Ukhti wa akhi

My grandma always tells me a story before I go to bed.

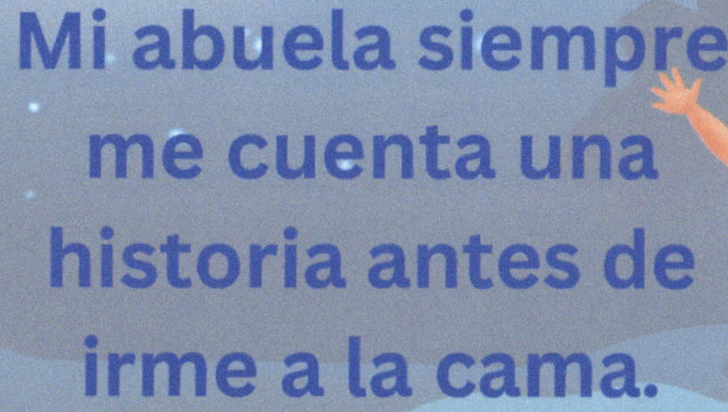

Mi abuela siempre me cuenta una historia antes de irme a la cama.

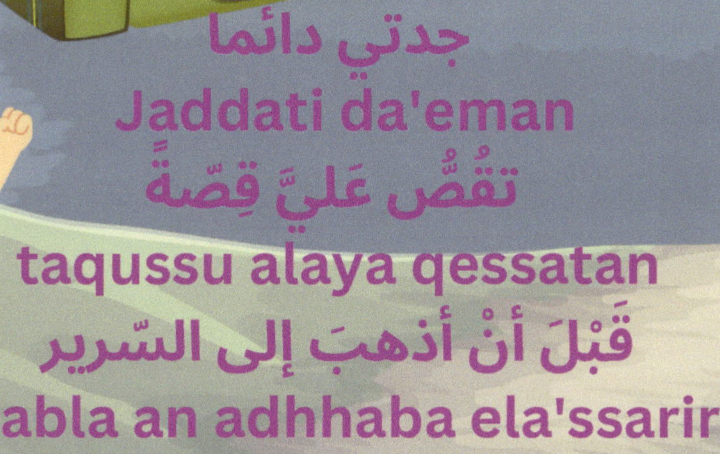

جدتي دائما
Jaddati da'eman
تقُصُّ عَليَّ قِصّةً
taqussu alaya qessatan
قَبْلَ أنْ أذهبَ إلى السّرير
Qabla an adhhaba ela'ssarir

All love to my
family. Mom, dad,
sister, and brother

Todo el amor para mi
familia. Mamá, papá,
hermana y hermano

كُلُّ الحُبِّ لأَسرتي
Kulu alhub le'usrati
ماما, بابا
mama, baba
أختي و أخي
Ukhti wa akhi

My grandfather and grandmother
My origin and culture
My mother is my embrace and my love

My father is my role model
My beloved ones
My brothers and sisters
Oh God, Oh God, Oh God
Save my family

Mi abuelo y mi abuela

Mi origen y cultura

Mi madre es mi abrazo y mi amor.

Mi padre es mi modelo a seguir.

mis amados

Mis hermanos y hermanas

Oh Dios, Oh Dios, Oh Dios

salva a mi familia

جَدّي وَجَدّتي
Gaddi wa gaddati
أُصْلي وثَقافَتي
Asli wa thaqafati
أُمّي حُضْني وَحَناني
Ammi hudni wa hanani
أبي قُدْوَتي
Abi qudwati
أَحْبابي
Ahbabi
إِخْوَتي وَأَخَواتي
Ekhwati wa akhawati
يَا الله, يَا الله, يَا الله
Ya Allah, ya Allah, ya Allah
احْفَظْ عائِلَتي
Ehfadh a'aelati

My body is my right
It's mine

Mi cuerpo es mi derecho
Es mio

Jesmi
huwa haqqi

Huwa lei

جسمي
هو حقّي

هُوَلِي

EAR
HAIR
EYE
MOUTH
NOSE
NECK
ARM
HAND
LEG
FOOT
I take care of my body and so do you.
Yo cuido mi cuerpo y tu también.
أَنا أَهتَمُّ بِجِسْمي
Ana ahtammu bejismi.
وَأَنْتَ أَيْضاً.
wa anta aydhan.

I comb my hair every day before leaving the house.

Me peino todos los días antes de salir de casa.

أَمَشّطُ شعري كُلَّ يَوْم
Umashetu sha'ri kula yawm
قَبلَ الخروج
qabla'lkhuroji
مِنَ المنزلِ
menalmanzeli

I brush my teeth after eating

Me lavo los dientes despues de comer

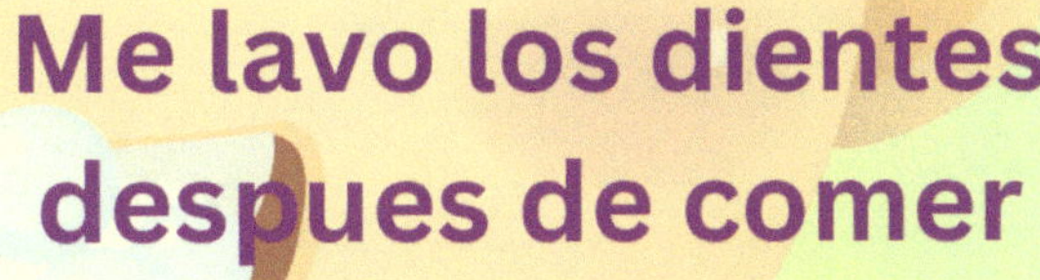

أُفَرِّشُ أَسناني
Ufarreshu asnani
بَعْدَ الأَكْلِ
ba'dal'akl

hand
mano
يَد
yad

face
cara
وَجْه
Waj'h

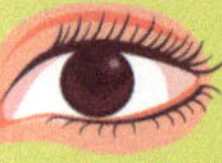

eye
ojo
عَيْن
ain

head
cabeza
رَأْس
ra's

tongue
lengua
لِسان
lesan

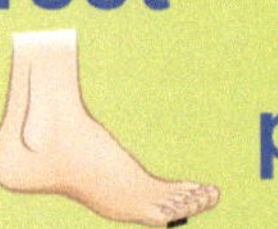

foot
pie
قَدَم
qadam

ear
oreja
أُذُن
uthun

nose
nariz
أنف
anf

knee
rodilla
رُكْبة
rukba

leg
pierna
ساق
saq

teeth
dientes
أَسنان
asnan

I can see with my eyes,
five fingers on my hands.

Puedo ver con mis ojos,
cinco dedos en mis manos.

astati'u an ara be'aini
khamsatu asabi'e fi yadaini

أستطيع أن أرى بعيني،
خمسة أصابع في يديني.

A big smile on my
face, when I see
you face to face.

Una gran sonrisa en
mi cara, cuando te
veo cara a cara.

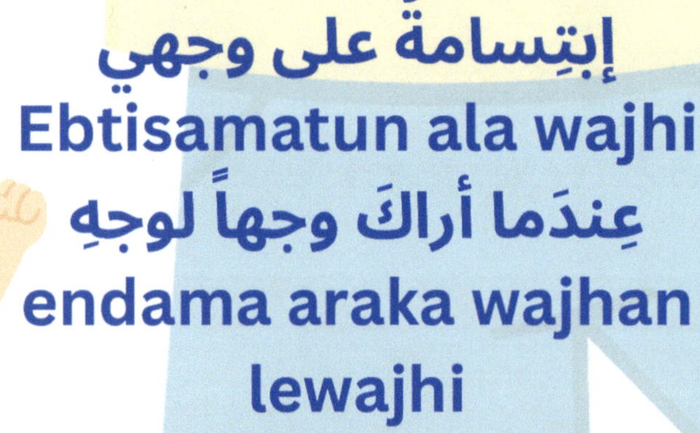

إبتِسامةٌ على وجهي
Ebtisamatun ala wajhi
عِندَما أراكَ وجهاً لوجهِ
endama araka wajhan
lewajhi

My face reflects my personality

Always confident in my ability

I feel shy sometimes when you compliment me

I am happy when I see you happy

Mi cara refleja mi personalidad

Siempre confiado en mi capacidad

A veces me siento tímido cuando me haces un cumplido.

Soy feliz cuando te veo feliz

وجهي يعكس شخصيتي
Waghi ya'kusu shakh'seati

واثق دائما من قدرتي
Wathequn da'eman min qudrati

أخجلُ أحيانا عندما تمدحني
Akhjalu ahyanan endama tamdahuni

وأسعدُ عندما اراك سعيداً
wa as'adu endama araka sa'eedan

Back to school

De vuelta a la escuela

العَوْدة لِلْمَدْرَسة
Al'awdah lelmadrasa

I go to school
every day.
My mother or
my father takes
me there.

Voy a la escuela
todos los días.
Mi madre o mi
padre me lleva
allí.

أَذْهَبُ إلى المدرسةِ
Adh'habu elalmadrasati
كُلَّ يَوْمِ.
kula yawm.
أُمّي أو أَبِي
Ummi aw abi
يأْخُذُني إلى هُناك
ya'khuthuni ela hunak

In my school, there are many classes and many pupils.

En mi escuela hay muchas clases y muchos alumnos.

في مدرستي كثيرٌ مِنَ الفُصول
Fi madrasati katheeru'mena'lfusol
وكثيرٌ من التلاميذ.
wa katheeru'mena'talameeth

Leo, escribo
me gusta estudiar
ciencias

أَقْرَأُ، أَكْتُبُ
Aqra'u, aktubu
أُحِبُّ أَنْ أَدرُسَ العُلومَ
Uhebu an adrusa al'ulom

Make a line.
Walk to class.

Haz una linea.
Camina a clase.

اعمِلْ صفاً
E'mal saffan
إمشِ إلى الفصلِ
Emshi ela'lfasli

Stand up,
good morning,
morning greeting

Levántate,
buenos días,
saludo de la
mañana.

إنهض, صباحُ الخَيرِ
Enhadh, sabahu'lkhair
تَحِيَّةُ الصّباحِ
Taheyatu'ssabahi

Sit down, listen to
me. Story of the
day

Siéntate,
escúchame.
Historia del
día

إجْلِسْ, إسْتَمِعْ إلَيَ
Ejles, estam'e elay
قِصَّةُ اليَوْمِ
qessatu'lyawmi

I am proud of what I have achieved at school

I wrote a lot
I read a lot
I learned a lot
I develop every day

Estoy orgulloso de lo que he logrado en la escuela

Escribí mucho

Leo mucho

Aprendí mucho

Yo mejoro cada día

أنا فخور
Ana fakhoor
بما أنجزته
bema angaztahu
في المدرسة
filmadrasa

كتبت كثيرا
Katabtu katheeran
قرأت كثيرا
qara'atu katheeran
تعلمت الكثير
ta'alamtu elkatheer
كل يوم أتطور
kula yawmen atatawaru

I love my school
My source of happiness

Me encanta mi escuela
Mi fuente de felicidad

أحب مدرستي
Uhebu madrasati
مصدر سعادتي
Masdaru sa'adati

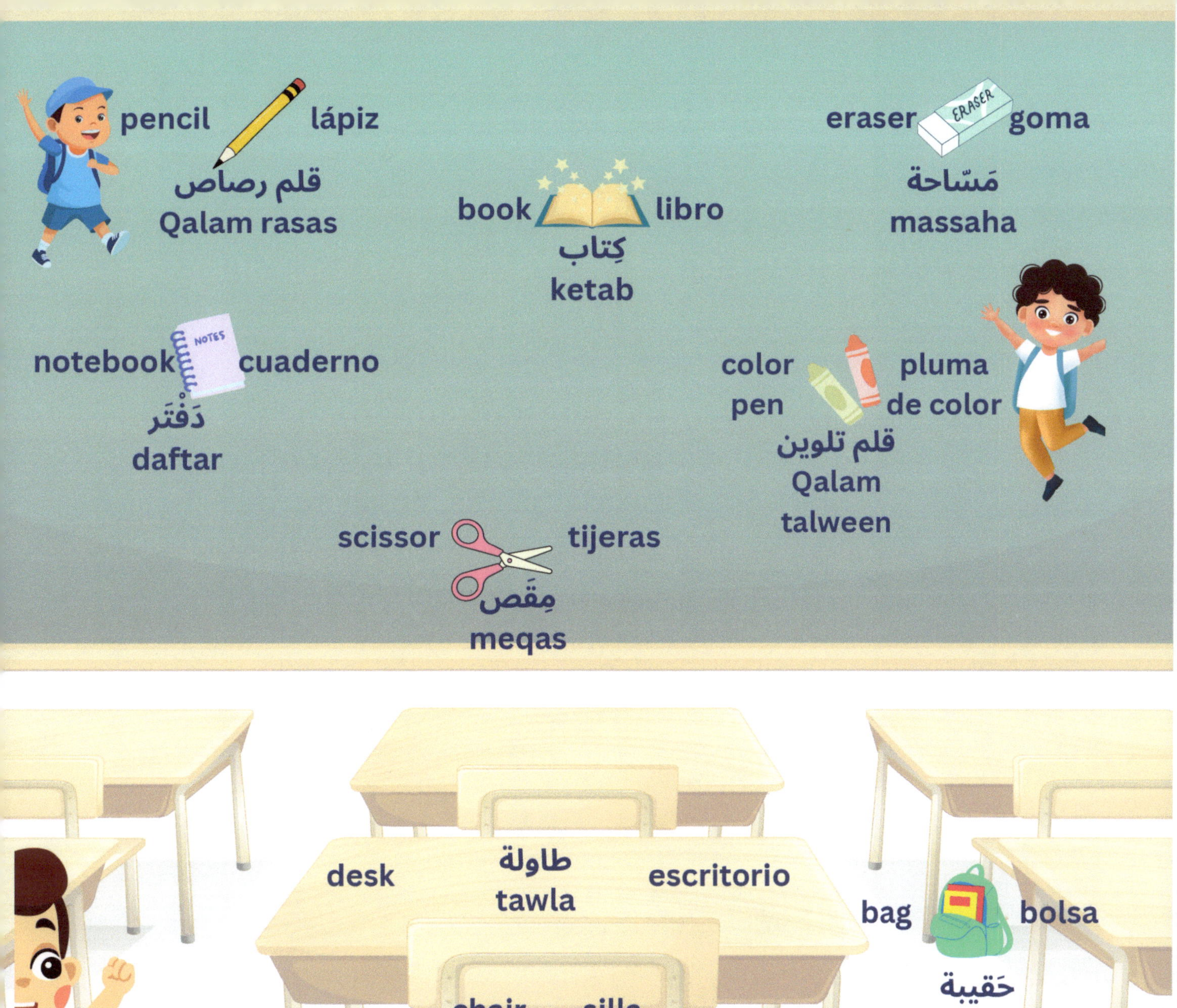

pencil lápiz
قلم رصاص
Qalam rasas

book libro
كِتاب
ketab

eraser goma
مَسّاحة
massaha

notebook cuaderno
دَفْتَر
daftar

color pen pluma de color
قلم تلوين
Qalam talween

scissor tijeras
مِقَص
meqas

desk طاولة escritorio
tawla

chair silla
كُرْسي
kursi

bag bolsa
حَقيبة
haqeeba

Good morning in the morning
Good evening in the evening
Good afternoon in the noon
And a good night of sleep
And a good night of sleep

Buenos días en la mañana
Buenas noches por la noche
Buenas tardes, en las tardes
Y una buena noche de sueño
Y una buena noche de sueño

صباحُ الخيرِ في الصباح
Sabahulkhair fi ssabahi

مساء الخير في المساءِ
masa'ulkhair filmasa'i

طابت ليلتُكَ عندَ النّومِ
tabat lailatuka endannawmi

Goodbye to you
Goodbye.
See you later

Adiós a ti, adiós.
Hasta luego

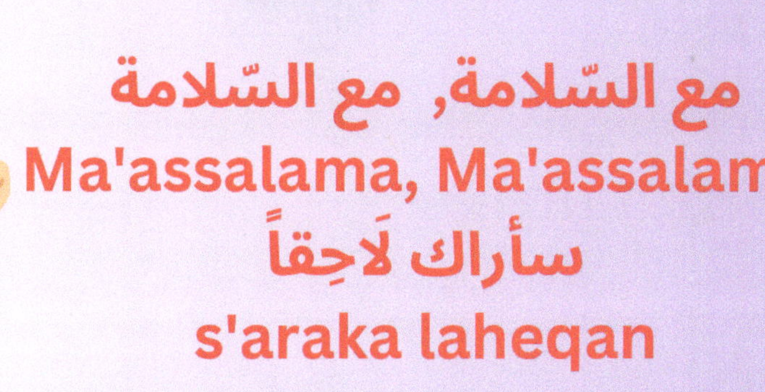

مع السّلامة, مع السّلامة
Ma'assalama, Ma'assalama
سأراك لَاحِقاً
s'araka laheqan

To be continued
in part 2 (two)

para ser continuado
en parte 2 (dos)

التَّتِمَّة
Attatemma
فِي الجُزءِ 2 (اثنين)
filjuz'e 2 (ethnain)

APPLE  **MANZANA**

تُفَّاح

TUFFAH

ORANGE  **NARANJA**

بُرتُقال

BURTUQAL

BANANA  **BANANO**

مَوْز

MAWZ

GRAPES  **UVAS**

عِنَب

ENAB

BLACKBERRY   ZARZAMORA

تُوت أسْود
TOOT ASWAD

STRAWBERRY   FRESA
FRUTILLA

فَراوْلة
FARAWLAH

WATERMELON   SANDÍA

بِطّيخ
BITTEEKH

PINAPPLE   ANANÁS

أناناس
ANANAS

CUCUMBER  PEPINO

خِيار

KHEYAR

TOMATOES  TOMATE

ظَماطم

TAMATEM

CORN  MAÍZ

ذُرَة

THURAH

CARROT  ZANAHORIA

جَزَر

JAZAR

BROCCOLI   BRÓCOLI

بروكلي
BROKLEY

ONION  CEBOLLA

بَصَل
BASAL

POTATO  PATATA

بَطاطِس
BATATES

LETTUCE  LECHUGA

خَس
KHASS

LION   **LEÓN**

أَسَد

ASAD

TIGER   **TIGRE**

نَمِر

NAMER

GIRAFFE   **JIRAFA**

زَرافَة

ZARAFA

ELEPHANT   **ELEFANTE,
ELEFANTA**

فِيل

FEEL

RHINO  RINOCERONTE

وَحيدُ القَرْن

WAHEEDU'LQARN

MONKEY  MONO

قِرْد

QIRD

ZEBRA  CEBRA

جِمار وَحش

HEMAR WAHSH

BEAR  OSO

دُبّ

DUBB

HIPPO  HIPOPÓTAMO

فَرَسُ النَّهْر

FARASU'NNAHR

FOX  ZORRO

ثَعْلَب

THA'LAB

WOLF  LOBO

ذِئْب

DH'EB

HYENA  HIENA

ضَبْع

DAB'O

TREE — ÁRBOL

شَجَرِة

SHJARAH

PALM TREE — PALMERA

نَخْلَة

NAKHLAH

GRASS — CÉSPED

عُشْب

USH'B

FLOWERS — FLORES

أَزْهار

AZHAR

www.ingramcontent.com/pod-product-compliance
Lightning Source LLC
LaVergne TN
LVHW071609180726
843512LV00003B/600